Stick Man

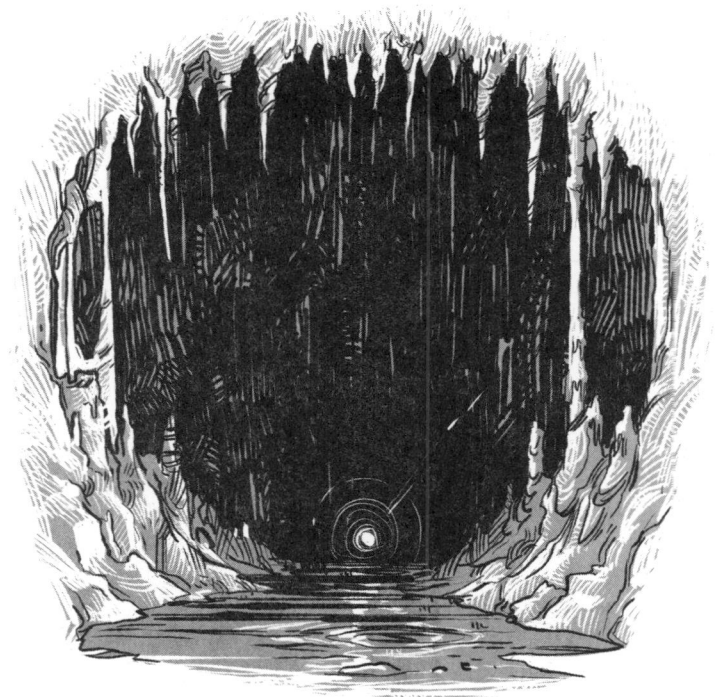

Written by John Lockyer
Illustrated by Mauro Mazzara

a Capstone company — publishers for children

"Look," Dev said to Kath. He pointed down the hill. "Grandad said that is Stick Man's lair."
"Stick Man's lair?" said Kath.
"Yes. A lair is like a den," said Dev. "Let's go and have a look."
"Must we?" said Kath. "It looks dark and wet."
"Come on, it will be fun," said Dev. "And I will tell you what Grandad said."

It was dim in Stick Man's lair so it was hard to see. There was thick mud, too. It splashed on Kath's legs and feet.
"Yuck!" she said.
"I will turn my torch on so we can see better," said Dev. "Shall we keep going?"
Kath nodded.

There were twists and turns in the dark lair.
Dev and Kath hopped across pools of mud. They stepped up into gaps. They jumped down off rocks.
They kept going. They chatted as they went.

"Grandad said far, far back, a man with a big stick lived in here. It was his lair," Dev said to Kath.

"And was he Stick Man?" said Kath.

"Yes," said Dev. "And he hid coins in here. He had a map. He put a big red X on it."

"Were his coins at the red X?" said Kath.

"Yes," said Dev. "But Grandad said Stick Man lost the map."

"Oh, that is bad," Kath said. "Did he get his coins back?"

"No. When the map was lost, the coins were lost as well," said Dev.

"Do **you** think there was a Stick Man?" said Kath.

"Oh yes," said Dev. "And Grandad said Stick Man is still in here looking for his coins. He taps with his big stick as he looks. He has a bright light to see by." Then Dev stopped.

"There is a lot of mud here," he said. "Shall we keep going?"

"No, let's go back," Kath said. "It's yuck in here!"
Kath turned to go out of Stick Man's lair. But then she said, "Um, how do we get out?"
Dev pointed to the left. "There," he said.
"No," Kath said. "We did not come from there. That mud is far too thick."

Kath said, "Keep near to me, Dev. I cannot see much in the dark."
"I will, but my torch light is not strong," Dev said.
They went to the right, but then they stopped. They were lost!

Just then ... **Tap!**
Dev jabbed Kath in the ribs.
"Ow!" Kath said. "What is it?"
Dev said, "Did you hear a tap just then?"
"No," she said. "I did not hear a tap.
Let's get going."

Tap! Tap!

Kath dug Dev hard in the ribs.

"Ow!" Dev said. It was his turn to jump.

Kath said, "I **did** hear taps!"

"Me, too," Dev said. "A lot of taps!"

They stood still. Ears straining to hear.

Then **Tap! Tap! Tap!**
"Oh!" said Kath. "Do you think it is a bat?"
"No," Dev said. "Bats do not tap!"
Kath said, "It might be a rat."
Dev said, "I do not think so."

Tap! Tap! Tap!

"I think it must be Stick Man we can hear!" Dev said. "Just like Grandad said!"

"Stick Man tap, tap, tapping with his big stick?" said Kath.

Dev nodded. "I bet he thinks we are looking for his coins. He has come to stop us."

"I think you might be right!" said Kath.

Tap! Tap! Tap!
Dev and Kath were afraid.
"Let's run!" Dev said.
They ran, but they did not get far.
Kath said, "How do we get out?"
But Dev just shrugged.

Tap! Tap! Tap!
"Oh no," said Dev. "My torch power is going down."
And then, the light went off.

Tap! Tap! Tap!

"The taps are nearer now," Kath said to Dev in the darkness.

"Then Stick Man must be nearer, too!" Dev gulped.

"It's so dark! Stick Man is going to get us," said Kath.

Then Kath pointed. "Here he comes!"
A bright light lit up the lair. It was hard for them to see.
"Oh no!" said Dev.

Tap! Tap! Tap!
"Run, Dev!" Kath yelled.
But Dev's feet seemed to be stuck to the spot.
He blocked the light with his hand.

Tap! Tap! Tap!
Then, there was Stick Man!
He tapped his long stick. He
held up his bright light.

"Get back!" Dev yelled at Stick Man.
He shook his fists.
"We do not have your coins!" Kath yelled.
All of a sudden, the light dimmed a bit.

"Dev? Kath?" said Stick Man.
"Grandad? Is that you?" said Dev.
"Yes!" said Grandad. "What are you doing here?"
"Looking at Stick Man's lair," Kath said. Grandad grinned. "But there is no Stick Man! That's just a bit of fun I tell my grandkids!"
"Oh, Grandad!" Dev said. "Then, what was all that tapping?"

"It was me looking for stuff," Grandad said. "I tap with my stick until I hit something."

Tap! Tap! Tap!

"See, here is something," he said.

"Is it a coin?" said Kath.

"No, there are no coins in here!" said Grandad. "Just lots of old tin cans. I put them in the bin when I get out."

Dev looked at Kath. "No coins, and no Stick Man. We are such fools!"

"Yes, what a load of old rubbish!" said Kath.